Published by Creative Education
123 South Broad Street, Mankato, Minnesota 56001
Creative Education is an imprint of The Creative Company

Art direction by Rita Marshall
Production design by The Design Lab

Photographs by AP/Wide World (Charles Rex Arbogast, Dennis Cook, Michael S. Green, Brennan Linsey,
Kim Truett), Architect of the Capitol, Corbis (AFP, Annie Griffiths Belt, Bettmann Archive, Najlah Feanny/
SABA, Michael S. Yamashita), Richard Cummins, Gerald R. Ford Library, Getty Images (Jason Cohn),
Harry S. Truman Library (Abbie Rowe, National Park Service), Jimmy Carter Library, Library of Congress,
National Archives and Records Administration, North Wind Picture Archive, Reuters (Hyungwon Kang),
Senate Curator (U.S. Senate Collection), Senate Historical Office, Office of Senator Strom Thurmond,
Unicorn Stock Photos (Chromosohn/Joseph Sohn, Patti McConville)

Library of Congress Cataloging-in-Publication Data

Fitzpatrick, Anne, 1978–
The Congress / by Anne Fitzpatrick.
p. cm. — (Let's investigate)
Summary: Explores what the United States Congress is, what it does,
and what daily life is like for senators and representatives.
ISBN 1-58341-262-X
1. United States—Congress—Juvenile literature.
[1. United States—Congress.] I. Title. II. Series.
JK1025 .F5896   2003
328.73—dc21   2002034866

First Edition

2 4 6 8 9 7 5 3 1

THE CONGRESS

ANNE FITZPATRICK

Creative Education

CONGRESS

American laws try to make sure that everyone has the right to "life, liberty, and the pursuit of happiness," as Thomas Jefferson wrote in the Declaration of Independence.

Above, the Declaration of Independence
Right, the writers of the U.S. Constitution

4

Laws affect our lives in hundreds of ways every day. Laws make sure the food we eat is safe and the water we drink is clean. There are laws that tell us who can drive a car and how fast they can go. Laws affect how toys are made and what's on television. Who makes these laws? And who put them in charge?

CONGRESS

M O T T O

6

GOVERNMENT BY THE PEOPLE

In the United States, laws are made by **Congress**. The men and women of Congress are the **elected representatives** of the people of the United States. They try to make laws that will be in the best interest of the most people.

Senator Bill Bradley talking to some of the people he represents

CONGRESS
SYMBOL

The bronze Statue of Freedom on top of the Capitol Dome depicts a woman holding a sword and shield and wearing a helmet crowned with an eagle's head, feathers, and talons.

Left, an illustration of the Revolutionary War Below, the Statue of Freedom

Before the American Revolutionary War began in 1775, Americans were governed by Britain. They were not represented in the government, but they still had to follow British laws. What made Americans really mad was that they had to pay **taxes**, but they could not tell the government how they thought the money should be spent. This was one of the main reasons they started the Revolutionary War.

CONGRESS

The American Constitution introduced new ideas about government. The people are governed because they give power to the government, not because the government takes power away from them.

CONGRESS

It took 17 weeks to write the Constitution. Many states did not think a Constitution was necessary, but only Rhode Island refused to send any representatives to help write it.

Many of the Constitution writers brought their families to Philadelphia

After the Americans won their freedom from Britain, they got together in the city of Philadelphia to form a new country. When they sat down to write the **Constitution**, they wanted to make sure that their new government would represent all of the people. They decided that each part of the country, called a state, would elect representatives to make laws. In order to make a law, a **majority** of the representatives would have to vote for it.

Some of the states were much bigger than others. The big states thought they should get more representatives. The smaller states worried that the big states would always get their way. They wanted each state to have the same number of votes in Congress. So the states compromised. Congress would be divided into two parts, called houses. One part, the House of Representatives, would have different numbers of representatives from each state, depending on how many people lived there. The other house, the Senate, would have two representatives from each state, regardless of the state's size.

CONGRESS
CHANGES

Changes to the Constitution are called amendments. The first 10 amendments, called the Bill of Rights, were added in 1791. Since then, only 17 additional amendments have been made.

9

A depiction of the Senate in 1850

*Although the
president is
the comman-
der in chief
of the armed
forces, only
Congress can
declare war
on another
country.*

10

The U.S. Constitution

The writers of the Constitution were worried about giving too much power to any one person or group of people. Many of them did not even want to have a president. They were afraid that he or she would be too much like a king or queen. But they also worried that Congress might become too powerful. They decided to create a system of **checks and balances** to make sure that no part of the government had too much power.

There are three branches of state government, too. Each state has its own Congress to make state laws, a set of courts to interpret state laws, and a governor instead of a president.

11

The system of checks and balances set up by the Constitution was made possible by dividing the government into three branches. The Senate and the House of Representatives are the legislative branch, which makes the laws. The president is the head of the executive branch, which makes sure that the laws are obeyed. The judicial branch, made up of the Supreme Court and the lower courts, decides how the laws apply to individual cases and whether they conflict with the Constitution.

Checks and balances make the U.S. government strong and fair

CONGRESS
TRIALS

*There have been only
two presidential
impeachment trials
in U.S. history.
Presidents Andrew
Johnson (1868) and
William Clinton
(1999) both won
their trials and
remained president.*

*Above, a ticket to the
impeachment trial of
President Johnson
Right, a House committee
debates impeachment*

he president can **veto** any law that Congress makes, and the Supreme
Court can throw out unconstitutional laws. This keeps the legislative
branch from becoming too powerful. Congress also keeps its eye on the
other two branches. Congress can vote to remove, or "impeach," the president
or a federal (national) judge from office if he or she does something wrong. The
Senate also votes on who becomes a judge. The president chooses the judges,
but the Senate decides if they should get the job or not.

The House of
Representatives
has 435 members.
California has the
most representatives,
at 53, and Texas
comes in second
at 32. Seven states
have just one
representative.

13

ELECTIONS

To be in the House of Representatives, a person must be at least 25 years old, a citizen of the United States for at least seven years, and a resident of the part of the state, called a district, that he or she is going to represent. Representatives serve for a term of two years and are all elected at the same time, on the Tuesday after the first Monday of November. Each state is divided into districts of about 600,000 people, and each district elects one representative.

Left, a billboard ad, part of a 1970s campaign Above, a meeting of the House and Senate

CONGRESS

LONGEVITY

Strom Thurmond, a Republican from South Carolina, is the longest-serving senator in American history. By 2002, he had been in the Senate for more than 46 years.

*Above, Senator Strom Thurmond
Right, Senator Hillary Clinton being sworn in*

A member of the Senate, called a senator, must be at least 30 years old, a citizen of the United States for at least nine years, and a resident of the state he or she is going to represent. Senators have a term of six years. Every two years, one-third of the senators are replaced or re-elected. There is no limit on the number of terms that a senator or representative can serve.

Most senators and representatives are members of either the Democratic Party or the Republican Party. These **political parties** help people to get elected. Once they are elected, the members of a party work together to get things done. Different parties have different ideas about what kinds of laws should be made.

The first woman in the House was Jeanette Rankin of Montana, appointed when her husband died in 1916. The first woman in the Senate was Hattie Caraway of Arkansas, elected in 1932.

15

Left, Democratic and Republican candidates starting campaigns Above, Hattie Caraway

CONGRESS
NAMES

Inside the drawers of each desk in the Senate chamber are carved the names of all the senators who ever sat there.

Right, candidates often walk in parades as part of their campaign Below, a Senate desk

Before an election, each party votes to decide who will run for the offices that are open. "Running for office" means trying to get elected. Then the Democratic **candidate** and the Republican candidate run against each other. There are also smaller political parties that have candidates, and independent candidates that don't belong to any party.

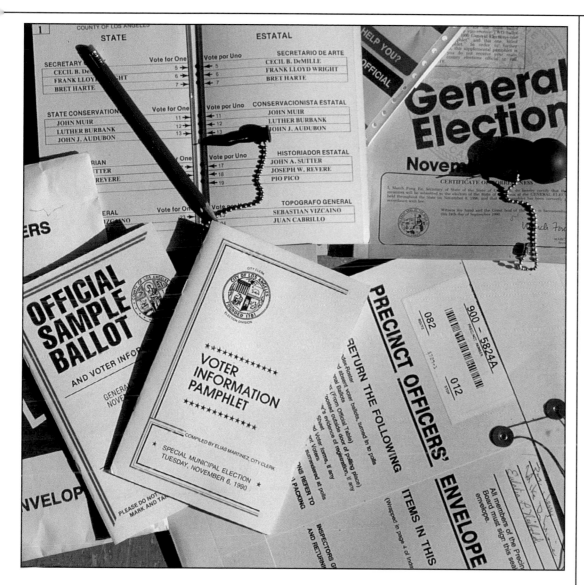

CONGRESS
H I S T O R Y

In 1870, Hiram R. Revels of Mississippi became the first African-American in the Senate. The first African-American representative was Joseph Rainey of South Carolina, elected the same year.

he candidates **campaign** to convince people to vote for them. On election day, all American citizens 18 or older can go to the polls—the official voting places—and vote for the person that they think will represent them the best. The candidate with the most votes becomes a senator or representative.

Many citizens vote using paper ballots like these

18

CONGRESS

HOME

The first meeting of Congress took place in 1789 in New York City. In 1790, Congress moved to Philadelphia, and in 1800, to Washington, D.C.

Scenes carved on the Capitol building symbolize freedom, equality, and justice

CHAMBERS AND SESSIONS

Congress meets in the Capitol building in Washington, D.C. There are two huge rooms, called chambers, where the Senate and the House of Representatives meet during a **session**. Senators are assigned to specific desks, with the newest senators sitting in the back. In the House of Representatives, there are no assigned seats. In both

chambers, the Democrats sit on the left side of the center aisle, and the Republicans sit on the right side.

At the beginning of each session, the representatives choose a Speaker of the House to preside over the session (to call on people to speak and make sure that everything runs smoothly). The vice president of the United States is the president of the Senate, but he or she usually comes only to the first day of the session. The leader of the majority party, the party with the most senators, presides in his or her place.

CONGRESS
ABSENCE

The president doesn't come into the chambers of Congress during debates. This tradition was started by George Washington, who was so well respected that Congressmen were afraid to disagree with him.

CONGRESS
LUXURIES

A renovation of the Capitol building in 1850 included the addition of bathtubs in the basement. Running water was still considered a luxury at the time.

CONGRESS

20

FIGHT

In 1850, Representative Preston Brooks of South Carolina began beating Senator Charles Sumner of Massachusetts on the head with his cane on the Senate floor after Sumner gave a speech opposing slavery.

CONGRESS

HELPERS

Teenage "pages" work in Congress as messengers. They live in a dormitory and go to school from 6:15 to 10:30 A.M. before going to work at the Capitol building for the rest of the day.

The president makes an annual "State of the Union" speech before Congress

During a session, members of Congress introduce proposals for new laws, have debates about laws that have been proposed, and vote on laws. The Senate votes by voice. Each member calls out "aye" or "nay" as his or her name is called. The House of Representatives votes electronically. Each member has a voting card, which he or she inserts into an electronic voting machine.

22

MAKING A LAW

In order to make a law, a senator or representative must first write a proposal. Someone from his or her home state or district might ask for a law requiring that people wear seat belts, for example. Or teachers might ask for more money for the schools. Once a member of Congress has written a proposal, he or she talks to other members to get them to support it. Then the proposal, called a **bill**, is introduced during a session of Congress. The member gives a short speech about why the new law is needed.

Children with diabetes attending a hearing for a bill seeking research funding

When the House is in session, the Mace is placed on the Speaker's desk. The Mace is a long silver stick crowned by an eagle perched on top of a globe.

23

Left, a citizen speaking to Senate and House committees Below, the House Mace

Next, the bill is sent to a committee. Committees are groups of senators or representatives who specialize in a particular area of government. A bill about seat belts, for example, might be sent to a committee on transportation, or health and safety. A bill about money for schools might be sent to a committee on education, or to a committee that decides how government money should be spent.

24

The committee may decide that the bill is a bad idea and toss it out. If they think it might be a good law, they have a **hearing** to gather information about the bill. The senator or representative who wrote the bill may ask people to come to the hearing to talk about why they need the new law. These might be people who were hurt in car accidents because they were not wearing a seat belt, or kids who go to a school that does not have enough money for books.

CONGRESS

PRESENTS

*Members of Congress
are not allowed to
accept expensive
gifts because they
could be seen as
bribery, but free
tickets to events
such as the Super
Bowl are permitted.*

If the committee approves the bill, it is then voted on by the whole Senate, or by the whole House, depending on where the bill was introduced. If one house of Congress votes in favor of the new law, the bill is then sent to the other house. The second house sends it to its own committee, and the bill is discussed and voted on once again.

*Representative Dennis
Hastert speaking in the
House chamber*

CONGRESS

AMENITIES

There are three restaurants, a barber shop and hairdresser, a dry cleaners, and a gym located in the Capitol building.

*Above, a congressman dressing for a ball game
Right, President Jimmy Carter signing a bill into law*

Finally, if the bill is passed by both the Senate and the House, it goes to the president. The president can sign the bill to make it law, or can decide to veto it. If he or she vetoes it, Congress can still make the bill a law if at least two-thirds of the members of Congress vote to make it law anyway. This is called an "override."

CONGRESS

TELEVISION

Everything that happens on the floor of the House or Senate is broadcast live on two cable channels: C-Span and C-Span 2.

Being in Congress is a lot of work. Votes sometimes take place after midnight. Members occasionally sleep on a couch in their offices and shower in the Capitol gym.

28

DAILY LIFE IN CONGRESS

Senators and representatives spend more time in committee meetings than in their chambers debating and voting. Even more of the meetings on a Congress member's schedule, however, are meetings with **constituents**, such as a union of factory workers or an organization such as Mothers Against Drunk Driving. Senators and representatives also spend a lot of time talking to the media, because this is one way that they can talk to constituents.

Members of Congress must find out what their constituents want

Members of Congress have a "franking privilege," which means they can mail letters to their constituents without stamps.

29

The hundreds or even thousands of letters, e-mails, and phone calls that a senator or representative receives every day must all be answered. Usually the Congress member's staff responds to the calls and letters. The staff makes sure that the senator or representative knows what his or her constituents are thinking and talking about. Once a week, all of the members of Congress have breakfast with their constituents. Anyone can go to Washington and have coffee, juice, and doughnuts with his or her senator or representative.

Senators are never too busy to talk with their constituents

CONGRESS
LIFE

Senators and repre-sentatives live in Washington, D.C., while Congress is in session, but they travel to their home states frequently to talk to constituents.

Senators and represen-tatives sometimes visit soldiers stationed in foreign countries

The job of every senator and representative is to make sure that the people he or she represents get their ideas heard. Citizens can help by paying attention to what is happening in their neighborhoods, throughout the country, and around the world. When something needs to be changed, a letter or phone call to a senator or representative can make a big difference.

CONGRESS

SCHEDULE

A session of Congress is held once every year, beginning on January 3. It usually ends on July 31, but the members can vote to extend the session if important business is not yet completed.

Glossary

A proposal made by a senator or representative for a new law is called a **bill**.

When people want to be elected, they **campaign** by giving speeches and talking to people to get votes.

Someone who is trying to get elected to the Senate or House of Representatives is called a **candidate**.

Checks and balances are limits placed on the branches of government so that no one branch has too much power.

Congress is the legislative body of the United States, made up of the Senate and the House of Representatives.

A Congress member's **constituents** are citizens who live in his or her state or district.

The **Constitution** is the document that outlines the United States government and how it works.

When someone is chosen for a position by a vote, he or she is said to be **elected**.

A **hearing** is a meeting held by a committee of Congress to gather information and opinions about a proposed law.

The greatest number of votes is called the **majority**. In Congress, the majority decides whether a bill becomes a law.

Political parties are groups of people who share similar ideas about how to run the country.

Representatives are people chosen by a group to speak for and to act in the best interest of the group.

A **session** is a period during which the members of Congress meet to debate and vote on bills.

Sums of money that citizens are required to pay a government are called **taxes**.

The president can **veto** a bill by refusing to sign it; this keeps it from becoming a law.

Index